Finding Skippy

Written by Michael Alcaraz

A real life Finding Nemo story about a dog owner trying to find his lost dog. This book is dedicated to my dog Skip and his brother Son.

Couldn't we agree that dogs are arguably the best creatures in the world? Ever heard the phrase "A man's best friend"? Some dogs have the curiosity of a child. They have the protection of a father and the souls of a pure mother. They can sense danger and look at us funny when we do something wrong. If they get in the way, we never really mind. John F. Kennedy once said, "My fellow Americans, ask not what your country can do for you–ask what you can do for your country." These days it's not about what our dogs can do for us–it's what we can do for our dogs!

Now some humans may be allergic to dogs or hate the neighbor's dog who always barks. A few may have got bit by a dog because the dog got startled and was being defensive of its owner. These incidents would create a negative association, but for the most part dogs are all good to their inner circle. Although we provide food and shelter to dogs and take them to the vet, they do far more for us. You can't put a price on friendship, love, accountability, or loyalty.

My name is Michael and I'm a substitute teacher for the middle schools and high schools in Wichita Kansas. I go by Mr. Alcaraz, Mr. A, Mr. Snitch, Coach, and some students know me as M-dawg. The district does a great job providing tools and resources for the students to exceed, but it's the choices students make that inhibit them from maximizing their potential. However, are they victims? Is it what they know from home? Is it from events in life that have shaped their character? Some just have a phone to stare at on the weekends and that is their dopamine. ADHD is at an all-time high. Some come from foster care, the projects, or abusive homes. Some have a ton of Jordan shoes and wear them off their parent's dime not knowing the value of a hard-earned dollar. Some students think detention is more fun than home. Is it the weird social phenomena's that go viral on social media that most of the youth eat up? Oh could it be a cause and effect from the video games they play or mumbo-jumbo music they listen to? Some students are only a few years younger than their parents. Recently I heard of middle school parents that are students at the middle school. Definitions of "be quiet" and "respect" are wildly different.

That's where I come in. They walk into the class and see me, a 27-year-old man instead of the average old lady or stern grown older man. I keep a beard so I don't blend in with the students. "You the sub?" "No, I'm just holding open the door because I'm nice like that." They read a quote, "What is your goal? Now multiply it by 10. If you fall short, you still will beat your original goal." I try to pump them up. I listen. I ask the questions they want to hear. I tell them "I understand" and I smile. I let them roast me. I roast myself so they don't roast each other. If they chose to be off task the first 10 minutes I let them play their game, but make it known they can't go to the restroom or get water till

2

they help me by doing their work. Somedays I'm asking for cell phones to be put away instead of taking them like other teachers that say, "Have your mom pick it up tomorrow after school," but fail to realize they take the bus. I sometimes break up fights getting ready to start and tell them to settle it on the handball courts after school. I love my job. Although I can't control the lessons the teachers want me to execute for the day, I demonstrate lessons through my approach hoping my positive behaviors will be modeled one day and last longer than test day.

I treat class time like it's a full-length football game. I fire them up halfway through like it's halftime. I tell them they are losing when they don't focus nor engage their brains. I fire them up the last 15 minutes challenging them to dig deep to finish strong, victorious, and with purpose hoping they can crank out a few more problems to please their absent teacher.

Nobody will remember learning about Napoleon, quadratic functions, MLA format, an animal cell, or Poe in grade school; these topics will not stick in the reality based world that we live in. However, they just might remember the stranger teacher that stuck up for them when they were getting bullied then gave them a couple bucks for a snack to eat out after school. Or they might remember the guy with a funky smile who chatted with them for 20 minutes and carried out a genuine conversation.

Today is April 18^{th,} 2016. I'm a PE Teacher at the
worst middle school in Wichita Kansas. I work a
half-day because I don't get much sleep the night
before. The school is surrounded by broken homes.
Some houses have boarded up windows, long dry
grassy front yards with chain linked front fences
that contain roaming pit bulls, cracked driveways,
and rusty basketball hoops.

During lunch, I throw a football to students on the
field. They don't see it coming from me, but I'm
launching 40 yard passes with accuracy through the
light breeze like I'm Tom Brady. Now other kids
want to join. As the ball soars through the air I
acknowledge the beautiful blue skies. It makes me
aware that I live in Kansas. This past December, I
moved 1,500 miles from California with a
masterplan that was slowly crumbling.

The bell rings and students head south to the
building. Two girls get into each other's space and a
small crowd starts hovering around. I jog over. "Do
something." I can tell both girls are scared. I enter.
"Break it up. No WWE!" and began separating
everyone in a nice way. Another teacher enters and
starts yelling at everyone to get to class. I walk
alongside one of the girls on the blacktop and say,
"I saved your life."

Back in the gymnasium, I supervise free play for the
next three hours. I always loved the game of
basketball, but basketballs as weapons are a

different story when you're a teacher. At times basketballs are thrown at students when nobody is looking. Some basketballs are kicked. Some punk student tries to be funny and throws a football towards my face but it barely misses smacking me in the face. If it did hit me, my loose aching wisdom tooth that is holding on by threads would have released and I would have screamed. I also don't have dental insurance. I'm in my second month of teaching and it's in this moment I learn a valuable lesson: bring a whistle.

I break up another fight. This fight is about a boy. One girl has tears in her eyes. I send one girl to the south side of the gym. The bigger girl with frizzy hair goes to the north side of the gym. They stare down each other. I hold a side conversation with a student as we sit on the bleachers, "This is fierce." Two students ask to go to the office to get an administration officer; they now have an excuse to temporarily leave my class.

Each class period goes by slowly and student safety is on high alert. Some student's think I'm cool, but I remind them that I'm not here to make friends. I'm drained and look forward to resting at home. I hadn't gotten much sleep as of recent.

I drive home. A deer sleeps on the side of the road and the savannah. The skies are still very blue and the clouds are white and picturesque. All I had to eat was a small bag of sour cream and onion chips so I contemplate eating something before my long-anticipated nap. Now back in the community, I park the car and expect the dogs to greet me with a sniff and a kiss. It's always so delightful.

I open the door and head up the stairs. We live in a townhouse. "Skip got out!" A voice comes from the patio. The kitchen and living room smells like cigarette smoke.

I pause for a second. "What do you mean Skip got out?" "He's not here anymore. He's gone." I start walking around the house with a sense of urgency. "What do you mean?" My voice breaks. "I have not seen him." My heart starts to race. I then start jogging around the house. I make sure anything with a door is opened. "TREATS!" "When is the last time you saw him?" "A couple hours ago." I ring the doorbell eight times knowing he will run out from where ever he may be hiding, but only Son barks. I hear and see nothing from house marsupial. Now I have a Bachelor's degree in English. I'm a critical thinker and my head does not leave the books. I might not have the best grammar, but I can think of an original idea. I search the two-bedroom house in about three minutes. Skip certainly is not home.

Skip, my princess, is a six-pound male Chihuahua we adopted back in the fall of 2011. He is tiny. His bones are brittle. He shivers and sleeps most of the day in a blanket or towel. He also has a low white blood cell count. This is bad, really bad. To think that he cannot be found is horrifying because he's smaller than your average Chihuahua.

I look at my other dog, Son. We adopted Son in 2009. Son is my son. Son is a Cocker-Spaniel-Shi-Tzu and has been by my side for eight years. It took me two weeks to finally give him a kiss when we adopted him. I gave in after he kept jumping in my bed in the morning. Son has a grey, brown, black, white shaggy coat. If you have ever looked into the eyes of a whale, you have looked into the eyes of this dog. I look at Son. He looks back at me with his under bite that no dentist will touch. I wonder if he knows his brother is missing? I wonder if he knows how Skip got out? I wonder what life will be for Son after losing a brother of six years?

I begin to panic and run outside. There is a light breeze. I start surveying the south-west side of the neighborhood. How did this happen? My brother has a mental illness so it's hard to get a straight story. Over the last month he had been a real pain. Budd Foxx was rude, disrespectful, and un-aware of how he was becoming a bad roommate.

Early in the month he got arrested for shoplifting at 4:30 am. I woke up to the cops knocking on my door. While in jail, I went through his dirty bedroom and found a bunch of salivated anti-psychotic meds tossed into the corner and bottles of alcohol purchased with money he had stolen from

7

me. My heart sank into my stomach and I fell into the wall. I knew I had a situation on my hands. Our parents live in California so this new battle was going to be all on me. At 5:30 pm, I pick him up from jail and try to convince him to go to the hospital for a little vacation. When we get to the hospital, he will not go in. After 45 minutes of negotiating, he makes a run for it. I start chasing him and he runs into a Vietnamese Café where a poker game is taking place. Budd Foxx says, "I put $5,000 on red." Everyone in the café does not speak English and look at as funky. I tell them to not pay attention and we leave. The scene outside is uncomfortable. He makes a run for it through traffic. I call the cops. They come and talk to us. I look at him from the distance and he's wearing a customized Miami Heat jersey with the last name "HANG EM"; I don't like to surmise but I believe he bought a visa credit card from the store, loaded it up with stolen funds of mine, and made the purchase. He's too smart at answering the law enforcement questions so they send us home. I drive home pretty pissed off knowing I have to feed him too. Later in the night, he starts knocking on people's doors at 11:13 pm. I call the cops so the neighbors don't call for disturbance. After analyzing him, they agree he should go to the hospital and they take him. Budd Foxx agrees that he needs a little help and asks to go on a ride-along. I celebrate after a long day then go to bed. At 3:07 am I get a call. "Michael, your brother has escaped from the hospital." My heart skips a beat. I call 9-1-

1 again and they only have three officers patrolling east Wichita. I lay down for a few seconds and realize that I need to become officer number four. It's 34 degrees outside and he's only wearing a hospital gown. I get dressed and head downtown which is 25 minutes away. I interview the hospital staff working the shift when he escaped to get a straight story. I check a local school, a church, a Denny's bathroom, and begin peeking into people's cars thinking maybe he thought it was too cold and found an unlocked car to sleep in. After a long night of searching around the neighborhoods of the hospital and driving alongside the half-frozen river channel, I come home knowing I have a long day ahead of me. I have to face my brother is dead, in jail, or in the hospital. At 8:19 am I get a phone call. I almost don't want to answer it. "Michael, your brother has been found naked in a McDonalds bathroom and is being returned to the hospital." I cry. So electrified from the news, I call my boss and tell him that I can work and that my brother has been found alive. When I get to the school, I accidently lock my keys in the car. Then in second hour, I give a speech to the middle school kids telling them something along the lines of "family is family and when a family member is going through a hard time, you stay by their side because in the end family is all you really have and the hard times shall eventually pass like the changing of the seasons."

The Notorious Budd Foxx had been banned from the YMCA, which I found out from another cop when he was talking to me as my brother was getting arrested outside our home for punching me and trying to stab me with a fork. Am I a snitch? No, my brother had been very wild so I was trying to build a case for his mental breakdown to get him long term help. Budd Foxx is Bipolar Schizophrenic and stopped taking his meds for a period of time. I'd like to believe his abnormal behavior was an effect from his meds taking time to re-integrate back into his biochemistry. He was chain smoking again after being off cigarettes for two years. He spent a few days in the psych ward and got released early after the big escape. I had been struck with random punches on a few occasions for no wrongdoing. Had my brother's recent madness gone over the limit? Even though Budd had been a headache, the anxiety in me wanted to believe that he would never hurt the dog.

I'd like to imagine that a wind draft caused the door to open and the dog got out because it was pretty windy earlier in the morning. Or my brother went on a walk, didn't shut the door, and Skip got curious and went on a walk of his own.

Here's the thing, Skip is the daintiest dog. The only thing going for him in terms of self-defense is his stubbornness. Every once in a while, he gets real rude, coils his lip, shows some little teeth, then strikes Son, causing his furry brother to cry. Son always has so much gook in his eyes because Skippy is a bully to him.

I check the washer machine, the furnace closet, and the outside dumpsters. I check a greenbelt behind a strip of homes. Nothing. I jog over to large plot of dryland that's two square football fields hoping to see a frolicking white dot. *Nothing.* I crouch down and think, "Oh my gosh! So much land!" I look take a spin. *Let's go!*

I go to the leasing office. "Hi Michael, how's it going?" They sense trouble because my brother had gotten the spotlight pointed on us from recent havoc in the neighborhood. The leasing staff is tired of residents not feeling safe because cops are at our house frequently. Stephanie, the head manager in charge, is over hearing about our downstairs neighbor complaints: slamming doors, cigarettes falling onto her porch and burning patio furniture, loud footsteps in the middle of the night. I was going to ask Stephanie on a date, but she learned I was bad and a leading member of The Notorious Alcaraz Brothers. Even the neighborhood kids had recently been scared off by my brother when he cursed at them from our upstairs patio. People pay a premium to live here and the community had really started speaking their voices against us. I walked into the leasing office tired, scared, and sad. Mike and Stephanie's body language read "nuisance."

"Has Animal Control been out today?" I explain the situation. "The little white dog?" "Yeah he got out. He's missing." They sense my pain. "Does he have a chip reader?" Now I feel like an idiot because that would come in handy in a time like this. Skip dog had no chip reader nor was he wearing a collar. Recently I took off the collar because I thought he looked cute without one. I beat myself up. *I'm such an idiot.* I also took it off because his collar rattling would keep me up at night. Him having no collar and not being a stray dog is a plot twist. If Son got out, someone would be like "Who's this cute dog? Oh, his name is Son. Someone lost their son."

Mike, the cooler leasing agent, grabs the golf cart and we cruise the perimeter of the complex. We cover more distance and have two sets of strong eyes. It feels like we can beat the traveling sun. Thirty-five minutes into the search I see no Skip. As Mike presses the pedal to the metal I looked towards the street looking for roadkill, fearing the worse. We vibrate over a field surveying the land.

As we zoom through the neighborhood, we stop and ask some elementary kids at the playground if they had seen the dog. I had never spoke to these kids but they see us on walks all the time. Son, Skip, and myself make up the neighborhood gang Three Dog Mafia. They had not seen the dog. Everyone probably knows me as the guy with two small dogs who keeps to himself and has the brother that stands out due to his all black attire, knack for trouble, and his grizzly bear body build. If they knew Budd Foxx like I know Budd Foxx, I would hope they would have some emotional intelligence.

Mike and I check the back roads. Where I live, you can see for a while. Kansas is flat and everything is spaced apart. *Why do I not see a scared dog who does not know how to get back home? Why do I not see a still dog with a red stained white fur coat on the side of the road.* Having peripheral vision and being able to see long ways, how do we not see him? Our eyes have covered so much ground. Is he trapped under an outside air conditioning unit? Did he get stuck in a patio closet? Did someone accidently trap him in their garage? The dog has a very distinct bark, but I heard no Skippy barks.

I come back home. Budd Foxx is smoking more cigarettes on the patio. I'm pissed. Why is he not helping me? Why does he not care? I call him out. He says "It's ok. Skip was a good dog, but you have always loved Son more." I'm more pissed and trying not to cry. I pray. Where is his emotional complex? I feel he knows critical information about Skips whereabouts, but I cannot interrogate him. He even tells me to stop interrogating him or he will call the cops on me.

I call my brother Nick who lives two hours away. "Little Skip is missing." "Oh no!" His girlfriend Mellissa over hears the conversation. He tells me to take Son on a walk to create a scent trail. My

13

daylight is precious and I have seen so much in so little time. I'm so pissed off I just want to talk to people who will care.

I call 9-1-1. They now have my information to notify me if they get any calls from local residents. The operator recommends sending a message to their page on Facebook so they can make a public post.

I get a knock on the door. It's Olivia, a young girl about the age of 12 from the brief playground interaction. She had heard from a lady who saw Skip. I follow the girl and tell her "If this leads to a discovery, I will reward you." I knock on the lady's door and begin immediately asking questions. "I thought the dog was my dog and when I approached her she ran away. I got in my car and tried to catch the dog, but she kept sprinting towards the dead end." The dead end she refers to is about a mile away. The anxiety in me believes that if someone were to pick him up, he would bite them and Skip would be euthanized for being a bad dog and I would get sued.

I imagine Skip being curious sniffing some green shrubs planted in dark bark. He knows he's doing wrong and should go home, but likes roaming around having complete control over himself. At the time of the day when this occurs, most everyone is still at work and kids are still in school. Sure, he probably drifted, but he had been on walks around the neighborhood plenty of times. Dogs are smart. Skip the ping pong head should know his scent marks and his way home because we go on nice walks all the time. Dog walks are my favorite past-time.

Maybe he was sniffing bushes and got scared as the complete stranger approached? The encounter causes him to become fearful and to lose his sense of exact location and direction. He bolts away in absolute panic. The lady tells me she chases after him because she fears he will get hit by a car. As he runs in the street I vision a white SUV traveling 10 miles per hour trailing him. He runs faster and faster fleeing for his life. He gallops through an intersection with cars nearing a stop sign. If a drone were to capture the scene from above it would film a car following a freaked dog. His black perfectly cared for soft paws pitter patter the warm black dirty pavement. His little paws are no bigger than my thumbnail; at home is only job is to keep his paws clean. Dirty paws = no chow. Skip's little heart wants to explode out of his small little torso. His 4-inch fox tail flaps. He knows the car is trailing him so he sprints as if he's "The World's Fastest Dog". Having respiratory issues, I'm sure he was huffing and puffing. Son on the other hand is slow, but is "The World's Strongest Dog"; he onetime moved a 25-pound kettlebell.

I know how fast Skippy can get when scared. Years earlier in the spring of 2012, I was throwing dog poop-pooh into the dumpster and a gardener was in the dumpster station. Skip pulled back and slipped out of his collar and took off like a bullet. In my other hand was Son, who had a cone around his neck from getting neutered a few days before. It was terrible timing and the gardener did not speak English when I asked him to hold Son, whom had been neutered a few days earlier. I ran after Skip, but Son was dragging me down. A stranger saw me in distress and said she would meet me back at my house 129 Huntington with Son. Cars would always speed in the project neighborhood of Orange County and I fear if I don't catch him soon, I will watch him get hit by a car in front of me. I was out of shape. I did cardio, but not this type of Olympic cardio. I have nothing left in me. My body is cramping. I'm crying. Skip is nowhere to be seen. I go back home. He shows up at the front door. I spank his little fanny pissed off, but so happy that he's back safe. I then pass out form exhaustion for two hours and when I wake up I have a stiff hamstring.

I know how fast he ran from this car on his tail. I now know that he has broken into a new horizon with new obstacles. If I was a true gambling man, I'd say he has no chance.

I sprint home, get in my car, and head towards the horse fields. There are bug infested trees, fallen leaves, a discarded McDonald's cup, and acres of land. I climb a barbed wire fence. It's the first time I had been over there since moving to the area. The terrain is dry. I look around calling Skip's name surveying the wasteland. I look down and my leg is bleeding. I feel no pain, probably need a tetanus shot, and keep searching. The field I wander is the perfect setting for an owl or Bald Eagle to scoop down and swipe Skip off the ground to feast for dinner. I'm a very fast walker so I cover the field at an abnormal pace. My adrenaline and focus is on a different level.

I hop over a small stream. It's a small stream that requires a little hop, but for the dog this would be a small challenge. The water is shallow. I imagine Skip taking a leap of faith to hop the stream, but judges his jump short. His lower body sways with the slow water current as his upper body struggles to pulls himself out.

My eyes survey the acres only to see nothing. The field is so dry and desolate, it seems like a prime setting for creepy crawly snakes to rover. I imagine walking up on a five-foot black venomous snake that has started feasting on Skip. I see Skip's dewclaws hanging outside of the snake's mouth as a small lump begins to decompress down the snake's body. Thankfully I do not come upon this disastrous scene, but if I did, I would be scarred for life because I am terrified of snakes. I probably would not even step on the snake. If Skip was only being suffocated, I would probably find a stick to smack the snake on the head hoping he would release the dog. Then I would sprint away, then juke the snake like I'm a football running back dodging a linebacker, scoop up Skippy with one hand and run for my life. I'm sure I would need counseling. Next time I'm at my brother's doctor appointment I would ask if they had a 2-for-1 counseling package.

I scope a different water channel with my keen vision. There is a film of algae and some rocks to walk on. There is no Skip but 50 to 60 geese and pheasants in the area. This leads me to an elementary school. I check the back lot and the parking lot. I've only covered a few miles, but I can see a lot further than I have covered.

I then drive around another neighborhood. People are starting to come home from work. I call Grandma who lives in California. All we can do is pray together. "Please bring little Skip home our Heavenly Father. This is too much for Michael to handle on his own. Give Skip the guidance to bring him home safe and alive." I have her on speaker phone praying as I drive around in my car now exploring distant territories. I tell God to bring Skip home. I get out of the car and check open backyards. Grandma is still on speaker phone. I know I am kind of trespassing, but I don't care.

I ask two joggers if they had seen the dog on their running route. They pull out their headphones, tell me they had only been running for 10 minutes, and wish me good luck. I usually run for 45 minutes so had thought they had been on a run for a while and maybe had seen a frazzled lost dog.

I pull into the YMCA parking lot. There are so many cars. The whole area is starting to get very busy. I walk into the gym. Pickup basketball games are starting. Two guys I know greet me like I'm checking into the gym for a workout, but today is different. I brief them and tell them to call the police station if any guest mentions a confused, distraught small white Chihuahua. The associate, Andrew, says, "Good luck! I had a small dog that got out once and got hit by a car." I say, "be thinking about me." They know I'm on a mission.

I walk back to my car and am horrified by the busyness of the area. I imagine a car turning the corner a little too fast. Skip braces for impact. The red lifted Ford Pinto brushes his ears as he crouches. A drop of hot oil singes Skip's fur coat, which causes him to shriek and nearly run into the oncoming back inner right 18-inch rotating rim and tire traveling at 15 miles per hour. Maybe the driver looks in the rear-view mirror and thinks "Did I almost hit a dog?" I think about me being the one to find Skip and he is on the side of the road, suffering, and his ribs are piercing through his skin and blood seeps out his nose as he has convulsions.

A personal memory comes to mind from when I was with my friend Shane and we hit a raccoon. The raccoon ran left, then ran right, left again, then we hear a major thump as we see panic in the coon's eyes. We scream for five minutes straight.

I'm Marlin from Finding Nemo searching for his son Nemo. I had always joked around calling my dogs "very feral" but who was I kidding? This is a horrendous situation. At this point, my perspective of loving Son more than I did Skip changes. Skip grew on me over the years. Our love took time, but inside I always felt like I leaned my love more towards Son which is terrible. It was probably 52% to 48% in favor of Son. Skip has sloppy kisses while Son's are more passionate. I realize for the first time that I love the dogs 50/50. They are equals and cause me so much joy and help alleviate my mild depression. At this point, there are only two guarantees. I guarantee that I will not stop searching until I have answers. I also guarantee that my dog has never been more scared in his life.

If Son goes on five walks a day, Skip goes on three. I cannot under-estimate how stubborn Skip is and if he comes home, he will be the King of the House for a very long time and can pass on as many walks as he wants. I'm at the point where I would love to let him poop and pee on the carpets in exchange for a safe return home.

Just this morning he woke up next to my head. As I struggled to get up, I kissed his little body as he coiled up like a cinnamon roll. Skippy peanut butter head puts his little paws on his eyes and nose because he is not only doing cute things, but he is being bashful.

I drive 750 feet back to the neighborhood that is kind of near my complex. I ask some folks chatting in front of their house with their neighbors if they had seen the dog. "No, but good luck." "If you see the dog call the police station." Mr. Kim is now on the line and shares some memories of Skip over speakerphone. "He had his issues, but he was an alright dog. Bring him home God. Bring him home our Father." I am at awe on how much territory I have covered. This search is getting more and more ridiculous as the sun heads west. We talk like we are police searching for a missing child. "10-4. If you hear anything let me know."

I head back home. By now, I had done three spiral checks. Each spiral getting wider and more intricate as I make my way back home. My phone rings. It's a restricted phone number. "Hello, Michael. This is Sheriff Dawn. Is your brother home?" "What happened?" "Your brother went onto a resident's patio and stole a pack of cigarettes. The resident was pretty freaked out." I imagine someone cooking an early dinner then they turn their head and see my 240-pound brother wearing all black tip-toeing on their patio to steal a pack of cigarettes resting on a small table. Or a little kid playing with toys and goes "Mommy, who is that on our patio?" And the husband sets his beer down, gets out of his Lazy Boy, and chases Budd Fox. This leads to a small chase and a verbal altercation. The resident ponders going to his locked safe to grab his registered pistol, but decides to alert the police. The guy describes my brother to the dispatcher and they know who he is referencing: good old Budd Foxx. I realize the cop car I saw about an hour ago was responding to a call about my brother. "They do not want to press charges. If it happens again he will get arrested for trespassing and theft." The conversation ends. *While I am out searching my heart and soul for our lost dog, he is stealing from the neighbors. Fantastic! His life, not mine.*

Budd Foxx gets in my car. I appreciate that he wants to help. He kind of has to help now. I can't trust him to be alone at home. "Skip." "Skippy." "Skip!" "Skippard Dean." We search and get out of the car. He starts to be annoying telling me that Skip is gone and had a good life. This is not the empathy and support I need, so I drop him off back home. This is terrible negative energy on top of an unfortunate situation. "If you get in trouble, I'm not bailing you out. Self-control, self-control, self-control!" I come home hoping Skip had returned. No Skip and Son can sense something is up. I retrace the beautiful beige and yellow Sun Stone apartment premises.

I check a local worksite and look down at the 10-foot hole in the ground that will make up a future basement. I step on wooden beams to avoid the thick mud from the rain on Saturday. I will rest when I have answers of life or death. It's that simple. This dog is my child.

Now I have about two hours of daylight left. Back to the distant neighborhood, I ask a group of kids if they had seen the dog. They said they had about 30 minutes ago and he was headed towards a park with a white gazeebo. I find the gazeebo they mention and search all around. I spend an hour looking around that neighborhood hoping this clue will bring me closer. *Can I trust these kids? I feel like a fool searching for fool's gold. Did I describe Skip accurately? Am I wasting my precious time?*

I talk to a guy on his porch as my eyes look around the man-made lake where the geese float. He tells me that his dog turned up in the grocery store parking lot numerous times. *Not a bad idea.* His loud dogs bark. I think of the fights and brawls Skip has probably been in today. Skip would be a rag doll for a big dog and an overpriced appetizer for a coyote or a Pitbull. Typically, when Skip gets mad at Son, his fur gets ruffled. I call him a "razorback" and wonder if he has been a razorback all day if he is still fighting. His legs are brittle like buffalo wings.

Being broke, I take my imagination to the what if scenarios? What if he has a broken leg? What if his eye is dangling out of his eye socket? I can't afford this type of medical bill. Am I now facing a lose-lose situation? I have been blessed to never have anyone in my immediate family die from sudden tragedy, but I sense today will live in infamy.

After 20 minutes of great searching, I exit the area and drive up and down the main road looking for road kill. At this point I keep asking God for help. "One more miracle. I need one more miracle God." I am now in a neighborhood with nice houses that has to be a 25-minute walk away from home. *How far did he go?* There is a small lake with no dog nearby. I tell myself, that it does not make sense for him to get this far.

As I drive to the Dillon's grocery store, I drive south on Andover Boulevard looking for roadkill. Every week I see raccoons, deer, squirrels, and opossums' dead on the road with a 50 mile per hour speed limit patrolling motorist. Will today be the day I see my dog on the side of the road, pancaked? Will there be a new spot that receives flowers to symbolize where life was lost? The old adage goes "The people of Andover do not know how to drive."

I walk into the grocery store after not seeing a dog in the parking lot. If I saw a stray dog off a leash, I would try to get its attention. I would know that this dog is in distress and misplaced from its owner. There's a sense of energy you feel knowing that you want your dog home as much as your dog wants to be home. Although dogs do not speak human, we know and understand one another to different levels. Skip is having the worst day of his life and mine is up there, probably top 3 worst days of my life. I feel so empty inside. I go to customer service, explain the situation, and tell them to call law enforcement if they come across Skip or if customers say anything about a stray dog roaming the parking lot. The pain I feel in my heart and gut is almost the same pain I felt when I broke my leg.

I go back home and send the Andover Police a message and some pictures of the dog. They post it on their Facebook. I don't share it because I don't want my mother to see my post. I go out for another search. The skies are very purple with tints of red. By now I am very hungry and cannot go any longer without food. I put a frozen peperoni pizza into the oven and set the timer for 25 minutes. I get back in my car and drive around with my headlights on. I figure I should go back to the houses where the kids said they saw him. *Nothing. Nothing. Nothing.* The street lights are on. I stop a person finishing up mowing their lawn to ask the question. *Nothing.*

I look towards the sky then tuck my chin. My cheeks pucker and a rush of emotions flows to my skull. "SOMEONE TELL ME WHERE MY DOG IS!" I rattle my arms in the air. The frogs near the waterbed and green grass croak. The fireflies light up. I punch the air.

After no sign of life anywhere, except for the busy streets with plenty of cars with their evening headlights on, I start to think about life after my dog as I come home empty.

I cherished our memories and was glad that we had spent quality time the day before. The day before was Easter. Budd Foxx, Skip, Son, and myself spent the day with our brother Nick in Great Bend. Skip sat on my lap for long stretches of the drive. As I drove, I rubbed his ears and paws. Skip was a lover and sat happily. I think about how God was with us on his day yesterday and it was a wonderful way to send Skip off to Dog Heaven. He never spoke to me in human, but I knew I was deeply loved.

I think about my mom. I plan on telling mom in a few days. He may show up in the upcoming days so I don't want to give her an anxiety attack. Mom has a big heart but overthinks. She lives in California and absolutely adores little Skip. Mom grew up with dogs, but gladly admits that little Skip was her favorite dog ever. My brother and I moved to Kansas back in November so she has not seen him in six months. My dad would not be to hurt by the news of Skip because he only met the dog a few times and always had his ankles attacked when he came to visit. I feel sad for my other dog, Son. Dogs are smart and I know he will forever be changed. I will retire Skip's leash and collar. I may even get his belongings framed.

Skip was an interesting dog and his death will be like a MH370 mystery. I'm sad and losing hope. I go to the oven and the only thing remaining from the pizza is the cardboard, a few peperoni slices, and sticky cheese. I'm speechless. I put my hands in the air in disbelief. Budd Foxx gives me a hug and I cry on his shoulder. "He doesn't deserve to die like this." "He was a good dog."

I start making flyers. *It ain't over till it's over.* I send a picture from my phone to my email. I Google lost dog flyers to get ideas. My phone rings. It's a number I don't recognize with a New York area code. I think it is my best friend Ethan. "Are you the guy with the missing Chihuahua?" My bones start to rattle. *Tell me more. What do you know?* "I think my neighbor found him. He posted something on Craigslist and told me that he had found a dog. I had seen the police post on Facebook. We matched the pictures and it's your dog." "Is he alive?" "He is alive!" I cannot believe what I'm hearing. My eyes are out of their sockets.

The kind lady and absolute stranger guides me to the Craigslist post over the phone. I can barely type and have tunnel vision. The page loads. It's little Skip. He has a gash on his head and ear, but is in good condition. Who knows if he fought a grasshopper, a frog, a snake, a branch, another dog, or a fence. Soon enough he would have been an a' la carte meal for perhaps an owl, a snake, a raccoon, a pheasant, or a coyote.

I rush over to the scene with Budd Foxx. I use my phone for a GPS. Soon I realize where we are going. These house's backyards are lined with massive trees, chain fences, and huge bushes that are like 15 feet tall. Man would need a machete to get through this mess.

It's dark and I'm in disbelief. Budd Foxx says, "Told you we would find him." We are greeted outside and escorted to Skip. I call his name. We make eye contact. He is coiled up and in distress. Skippy slowly comes out from under a small bench under a porchlight. He looks terrified, but at peace in the matter of two seconds. His ear has a small gash, but it doesn't look too serious. Maybe he got in a rumble with a field mouse? Or maybe he fought off a squirrel in a punching bout or got cut going under a fence. I will never know. I pick him up. "What in the hell happened?" Skip is shaking. He is beaten and battered. He is unaware of what he just did.

"How did this all come about?" The gentleman tells me that his dog started barking and would not stop. "I finally got annoyed and went to see what was the matter. When I realized he was barking at small dog, I grabbed a bucket to try to catch him and he took off running and ended up under this bench." The man had put food and water out.

Although I could not offer much, I gave the two helping parties a copy of a book I wrote, *The Book*

Of Muh, The Not Funny Joke Book. I shake five
people's hands including the little kid's standing
around on the grass. It was the least I could do
considering I could not offer much and was now
forever in debt.

I add the clues up and calculate that Skip had
traveled maybe 1.5 miles. He had gone through
different kinds of terrain, maybe a small stream,
backyards, and busy traffic. Skip is so feral, I jump
up and down. Where he was found is very far from
the clues I had been given. He was easily a 30-
minute human walk from home. To a Chihuahua the
size of a shoe, this is much further.

The three of us celebrated by getting milkshakes.
Skip sits in my lap as we sit in the carhop at Sonic. I
put some of my strawberry shake on my finger and
let the dog legend lick it. I call Nick and Grandma.
We are rejoicing in hallelujahs.

When I got home, Son sniffs Skip; it was him. The
dog is too tired to make it up the stairs so I carry
him and put him on some towels. In my room and
on my bed, Skip passes out from exhaustion. I call
more family and friends to celebrate. I let Skip
catch his breath to realize that he is back home and
alive! I call my mom to tell her about the events that
had unfolded. She is speechless.

I give my little Skippy a bath. First, I wash him
gently with warm water then I cover his eyes and

pour hydrogen peroxide on his cut. A trail of faint blood streams down his face. Then I wash him with Dawn soap pretending he is a little duck being rescued and washed after getting caught in an oil spill. I scrub tree sap off his feeble legs and arms. I scrub the gook caused from tears out of his eye sockets. His body aches. He is home. "What the hell happened? Please tell me what in the hell happened?" I'm in shock as I look my dog into the eyes. He's possessed. He has seen things that he didn't want to see. I look deeply into his eyes and they are very different from this morning and he will never be able to tell me what happened because he's a dog. I diagnose him with PTSD. Skip faced death and survived. I will never know how many times my boy avoided death, but I know he's back in my possession. *I wonder if he outran squawking geese?* I dry him off from head to paw. He sneezes. I fluff my blanket and make him a nice bed for the evening.

Now with Son, I let Skip sleep. We go on a walk around the neighborhood loop and I pray to God thanking him for his mighty hand to bring Skip home to safety. The toads are out hopping around. It dawns on me why he survived. He had prayer, the mighty Holy Spirit driving him every direction he went, to break down every obstacle in his way. Raccoons, squirrels, armadillos, deer and other wild animals end up sleeping on the side of the road because they didn't have a prayer team sending them home to safety. They didn't have the powerful

Lord saying, "Stop here my child and let this car pass."

For a day, although I may never know the true story on how he got out and what he endured to survive, Skip was a little warrior. I take a shower and watch dry blood, dirt, and grime rinse off my tired legs. I peak outside the curtain to look at my Skippard-Dean. He's no longer a Chihuahua, he's a domestic coyote.

Thank you for reading this incredible true story. If Skip's warrior spirit touched your heart, please share this book with friends, family, and animal lovers. If you would like to book Skip and myself for speaking engagements focused on the theme of "courage" please email me at themichaelalcaraz90@gmail.com. We are even considering movie options that may come to the table. Also fill free to check out my website: michaelalcaraz.wordpress.com.

Lastly, if you enjoyed the cover artwork, give @echandl2 a follow on Instagram.

www.ingramcontent.com/pod-product-compliance
Lightning Source LLC
Chambersburg PA
CBHW060547030426
42337CB00021B/4473